# You Can Write a Terrific Opinion Piece

by Jennifer Fandel

Consultant:
Terry Flaherty, PhD
Professor of English
Minnesota State University, Mankato

CAPSTONE PRESS
a capstone imprint

First Facts is published by Capstone Press,
1710 Roe Crest Drive, North Mankato, Minnesota 56003.
www.capstonepub.com

Library of Congress Cataloging-in-Publication Data
Fandel, Jennifer.
  You can write a terrific opinion piece / by Jennifer Fandel.
    p. cm. — (First facts. You can write)
  Includes index.
  Summary: "Introduces readers to the key steps in writing an opinion piece
through the use of examples and exercises"—Provided by publisher.
  ISBN 978-1-4296-8409-5 (library binding)
  ISBN 978-1-4296-9316-5 (paperback)
  ISBN 978-1-6206-5259-6 (ebook PDF)
  1. Journalism—Authorship—Juvenile literature. 2. Newspapers—Sections,
columns, etc.—Juvenile literature.  I. Title.

  PN4784.C65F36 2013
  808.06'607—dc23                                          2012003764

**Editorial Credits**
Jill Kalz, editor; Sarah Bennett, designer; Kathy McColley, production specialist

**Photo Credits**
Capstone Studio: Karon Dubke, 6, 8; iStockphoto: Csaba Vanyi, 24, Csaba Vanyi, cover (red
rabbit), Sean Locke, 11; Shutterstock: Darrin Henry, 17, irin-k, cover (pencils), Jagodka, 10,
18, 19, Joy Brown, 21, kkays2, 12 (background), Mariia Sata, 9 (beach), michelleannb, 13,
Monkey Business Images, 5, R. Peterkin, 9 (mountains), RDTMOR, 7, Shebeko, 16, Stefan Petru
Andronache, 12 (rabbit), Stefan Petru Andronache, cover (brown rabbit), Victoria Rak @ Tuff
Photo, 15, vovan, 16

**Artistic Effects**
Shutterstock: bogdan ionescu

Printed in the United States     5571

# TABLE of CONTENTS

# For or Against

Are school uniforms good or bad? Should you get paid for walking the dog? Does your town need a new park?

There are two sides to every **issue**. You are either **for** something or **against** something. The side you take is your **opinion**. Everyone has opinions. There are no right or wrong opinions.

**issue**—an idea or need that is talked about

**opinion**—a person's ideas and beliefs about something

POSITION

Opinions are not the same as likes and dislikes. "I like pizza" isn't an opinion. Saying "Guido's Pizza is better than Rico's Pizza" is an opinion. You are stating a **position** that you can support with proof. You can show people why one pizza place is better than another.

**position**—a person's point of view on an issue or subject

Write down five opinion questions that begin with "Do you think." Then state your position on each.

Do you think fish make good pets?

Do you think Superman could beat Batman?

Do you think winter is better than summer?

Do you think you need a new bike?

Do you think you should go to school on Saturdays?

**FAST FACT**

Opinions are different from facts. "Earth is round" isn't an opinion. It's a fact. Facts do not have two sides. They are truths.

Before you start an opinion piece, know why you're writing it. Have a clear purpose. Do you want to change readers' minds? Do you want them to take action?

**My Position:**
Mom and Dad should let me get a pet rabbit.

**Purpose:**
To show Mom and Dad I can be a trusted pet owner

**Audience:**
Mom and Dad

Also, know your **audience**. You talk to your teachers differently than you talk to your friends. Choose words that fit your audience.

**audience**—the people to whom you're speaking

Pretend this is your opinion: A trip to Florida is better than a trip to Alaska. What might your purpose be for writing about this? Maybe you want your parents to change the family vacation. Maybe you want your aunt to buy you a new beach towel. What other reasons might you have?

# INTRODUCTION

An opinion piece starts with an **introduction**. An introduction explains the issue. It tells why the issue is important. State your position clearly. Start with words such as "I think" or "I believe."

All of my friends have pets. I've always wanted a pet rabbit. I think I could take good care of a pet.

**introduction**—the beginning of an opinion piece

# Exercise

Choose a school issue you care about. Maybe you believe your school needs a new theater. Maybe you think more fruit should be served at lunch. Write an introduction about the issue.

Jefferson School needs a new theater. It needs a new gym too. But the school has money for only one. I believe the school should choose the theater.

The best opinion-piece writers listen. They listen to what people on the **opposite** side of an issue say. If you know what their reasons are, you can better prove your opinion. Think like the opposite side.

Opposite Position:
My child should **not** get a pet rabbit.

Reason 1:
My child won't take care of a pet.

Reason 2:
Pets cost a lot of money.

**opposite**—as different as possible

12

# Exercise

Pretend this is your opinion: I should be paid for doing chores. What might the person on the opposite side say? What reasons might he or she give for *not* paying you? List at least three reasons.

13

## Build Support · PROOF

Now turn the other side's reasons into support for your opinion. Prove that the other side's reasons are not as strong as yours. Start by stating the other side's first reason. Answer it with your own reason or reasons.

Opposite Reason 1:
My child won't take care of a pet.

Your Reason 1:
I water the plants.

Your Reason 2:
I do chores without being asked.

Your Reason 3:
I take care of our class pet.

Then connect these ideas with a word or words that show **contrast**.

**contrast word**

All of my friends have pets. I've always wanted a pet rabbit. I think I could take good care of a pet.
Mom says I won't take care of a pet. However, I do a lot of work without being asked. I water the plants. I do chores. I also take care of our class hamster.

**contrast**—a difference

# EXAMPLES

Reasons **tell** readers information. Examples **show** it. Examples make reasons stronger. Try to include examples for all of your reasons.

anted a pet rabbit. I think I could take good care of a pet.

Mom says I won't take care of a pet. However, I do a lot of work without being asked. I water the plants. I do chores. I also take care of our class hamster.

I've watered the plants all year. All 10 plants are healthy. So is our class hamster.

In the sample piece, you say you water the plants. But how long have you been doing this? How many plants are there? Are they healthy? Show your readers how you take care of the plants.

Pretend this is your reason: I am a good student. To show how you're a good student, you might use these examples: I get to class on time. I do my homework. I'm polite to my teacher.

Now give at least three examples for this reason: I help people. Show *how* you help others. What do you do?

## No Right or Wrong

No one likes a cheater, so be fair. Use only the opposite side's best reasons for your opinion piece. It's not fair to pick weak reasons to make your reasons look stronger.

Also, don't bully readers. Remember, there are no right or wrong opinions.

# Exercise

Cats are unhappy animals, so dogs make better pets.

Is this sentence about cats fair? How do you know all cats are unhappy? Instead try this: Dogs make better pets than cats because dogs are usually easier to walk.

Everyone who is smart knows that dogs are better pets.

How do you think this sentence makes cat lovers feel? Reword it to remove the bullying.

FAST FACT
You can find opinions in newspapers. Sometimes people write letters to the editor. The writers share their opinions on issues important to them.

## Say It Again!

In the **conclusion**, restate your purpose. Repeat your position. And leave readers with something special to remember. It might be thoughtful, sweet, or funny.

All of my friends have pets. I've always wanted a pet rabbit. I think I could take good care of a pet.

Mom says I won't take care of a pet. However, I do a lot of work without being asked. I water the plants. I do chores. I also take care of our class hamster.

I've watered the plants all year. All 10 plants are healthy. So is our class hamster.

Dad says pets cost a lot of money. But I can use my birthday money to buy a rabbit. I can shovel snow to earn money for pet food.

**Mom and Dad, you should let me get a rabbit. I will take good care of it and help pay for it. And rabbits don't bark!**

**conclusion**—the ending of an opinion piece

You've got lots of opinions. Write them down and share them!

# GLOSSARY

**audience** (AW-dee-uhns)—the people to whom you are speaking

**conclusion** (kuhn-KLOO-shuhn)—the ending of an opinion piece

**contrast** (KAHN-trast)—a difference

**introduction** (in-truh-DUHK-shuhn)—the beginning of an opinion piece

**issue** (ISH-oo)—an idea or need that is talked about

**opinion** (uh-PIN-yuhn)—a person's ideas and beliefs about something

**opposite** (OP-uh-zit)—as different as possible

**position** (puh-ZISH-uhn)—a person's point of view on an issue or subject

# READ MORE

**Fields, Jan.** *You Can Write Great Letters and E-mails.* You Can Write. North Mankato, Minn.: Capstone Press, 2012.

**Purslow, Frances.** *Persuasive Paragraphs.* Learning to Write. New York: Weigl Publishers, 2008.

**Throp, Claire.** *Put It Together: Using Information.* Our World of Information. Chicago: Heinemann Library, 2010.

# INTERNET SITES

FactHound offers a safe, fun way to find Internet sites related to this book. All of the sites on FactHound have been researched by our staff.

Here's all you do:

Visit *www.facthound.com*

Type in this code: 9781429684095

# Index